Busy Girl's Guide to Happiness

Happiness, Simplified

KRISTINA D. TSIPOURAS

www.busygirldaily.com

KRISTINA D. TSIPOURAS

ISBN: 978-1530-977253
ISBN-10: 1530977258

DEDICATION

This book is dedicated to my Yia-Yia and Papou
The two happiest souls I have ever known.

KRISTINA D. TSIPOURAS

CONTENTS

ACKNOWLEDGMENTS

I have had two amazing spiritual mentors in my life
that truly stand out. These two women changed my life
and I will continue to be thankful to them forever. I
wanted to specifically acknowledge Asha Ramakrishna,
my spiritual coach who I worked with for many years.
If you may be interested in taking any of the practices,
rituals or theories that I discuss in this book a step
further, may I recommend checking out:
ashaisnow.com for more information.

KRISTINA D. TSIPOURAS

INTRODUCTION

Happiness defined

"Bliss cannot be disturbed by loss or gain." - **Yogi Tea tag**

Hello fellow Busy Girls! My name is Kristina and I am a 31-year-old entrepreneur living and loving life in Boston, Massachusetts. Over ten years ago, I started my journey to finding happiness and becoming the best version of myself.

I have read hundreds of books, have been mentored by some of the best, have gone to every seminar you could imagine, and have tried out every 'self-help' practice available. I was always eager to learn more, to be more, to have more, and to find more and I would stop at nothing to reach my fullest potential and find true happiness!

To find inner peace and happiness, while still relating to every girl, I decided to write, *The Busy Girl's Guide to Happiness.* This book represents the short and simple version of the long self-help journey I found myself on. It breaks down the best advice, guidance, and tools I received along the way. The cliff-notes to Happiness, if you will. Yes, I was that rebel in high school who only read the cliffs-notes!

I am not your typical spiritual yogi. I love fashion, I love the freedom and extravagant life that money and success allows me. I also loved being part of a sorority

(Delta Delta Delta), wearing pink lipstick and I do love my leopard print! You don't have to be barefoot with dreadlocks to consider yourself a spiritual person.

There are so many mentors I've looked up to that I could not personally relate to. They didn't look like me, or talk like me. They didn't read Vogue every month, or value the same type of lifestyle that I did. So this is for you, my fellow fashionistas, fellow busy girls, and fellow every girl. It's time to make the journey to happiness more fun, easy, accessible, fashionable, and even sexy. I want to start by welcoming you to the tribe, fellow busy girl. It is time to start your journey to happiness! Join me and other busy girls on this journey by using the hashtag #busygirltribe on social media. I want you to feel supported and understood, and I want you to have an everyday reminder in your newsfeeds that you are not alone. The tools in this book are the most powerful that you may ever come across, so buckle up and get ready to change your life.

Now before we dive in, I want to take a moment to honor you and the work that you will do here. You should be so proud to have made it so far. Just think about how much you have already overcome, and how much is waiting for you just over the horizon. To begin, I would like you to take the term 'self-help' out of your dictionary. Let's approach this as 'upgrading yourself'. Just as you would upgrade your wardrobe, salary, career, life partner, and the people you surround yourself with. You have made a choice to upgrade yourself. You have chosen to invest in yourself, so kudos to you. You are already ahead of the gang!

Happiness is yours to own, so let's begin!

To begin, I am going to challenge you to change your current belief system and to take control of your thoughts. A belief is simply a thought that you keep thinking. So if you want to change your belief system, then you must change your thoughts. We have control over our thoughts and over our mind. It takes patience and practice to be able control your thoughts, and to not let your them control you, but it does work.

Start here: You don't have to buy into every thought that you think. If some of your thoughts aren't serving you, then let them go! Only follow thoughts that make you feel good. Often, negative thoughts are simply a false reality. You see, our feelings are a good indicator of whether or not we are on the right track. So if you are feeling negative about a thought, it may give you peace of mind knowing that a negative feeling only means that you are thinking about something that isn't true to you.

We are going to go deep here, but there are two strong concepts I learned over the years that have helped me to deal with difficult people. Whether it is in friendship, in love, or in business, it will help you find compassion and understanding for the most difficult people you come across. As a result, these situations will be a bit easier to navigate through, which will make difficult situations and dealing with difficult people easier and even more enjoyable when you make them about yourself! Drop the drama and take it inwards, make it only about you, your growth, and how you will be stronger for getting through it.

Challenging people and situations are brilliant gifts. They are there to teach you, to allow you to grow and become better and stronger. I have found that the most enlightened people have generally gone through the most difficult situations. Trust and allow the universe; it's trying to close a door for you so that a new one can open and you can walk through it without any resistance. Remember, every situation in your life is happening for you, not to you.

BUSY GIRL ACTIVITY 1

The Happiness Contract

In order to be a successful busy girl, you have to start here. You have to make a promise to yourself to make happiness (and positive thoughts) your number one priority. Before reading this book, or going any further, I want you to take out a piece of pen and paper, or open up your laptop and write a contract to yourself, or you can copy and paste this contract (found on busygirldaily.com)

Busy Girl contract:

I (add your name) _____ , a successful busy girl vow to be true to myself every day. I promise to speak my truth, live my truth, and make an effort to find good feeling thoughts, and positivity in every situation, and in every day. I promise to not let my feelings; thoughts and emotions take control of me, or deter me on my path to success. I promise to put my feelings and my needs first, above everything else. I understand that in doing so my life will get better, I will get better, and I will be able to better support everything and everyone in my life.

I promise to keep a daily journal of positivity, and remind myself that this will be an amazing journey, if I let it be. I plan to work on making sleep, exercise, and healthy eating priorities in my life. I promise to change my life and myself for the better. I will re-establish my thoughts, my habits, and my foundation, and make lifestyle changes that I can implement and live by for the rest of my life. Today, I raise the standards for myself, and my happiness.

I love you (insert your name here) _____, I love you Universe, I have everything I need within me. Starting today, I am my top priority.

Date _____

(Your signature) _____

(Keep this in a journal by your bedside table, or on your desk at work, or on your bathroom mirror. Promise to read it to yourself every morning or every night.)

PART 1

Where To Begin

"Happiness is when what you think, what you say, and what you do are in harmony." - **Gandhi**

1. The Power of Positive Thinking

"The Grass is greener where you grow it" - **Unknown**

My first year of college was the worst year of my life. The school I chose was the wrong one for me. I didn't feel connected to anyone I met, and my entire support system was a plane ride away. I was trying to hold on to a long distance relationship with my boyfriend of three years and was just absolutely miserable. I felt depressed, so I decided to make an appointment with a college counselor. In our first session, she told me something that I didn't realize would change my life forever.

She said, "You have power and control over your thoughts. When you start to think happy thoughts, you will feel happier, and then when you start to feel happy, you will become happy. In any situation, you can trick yourself into being happy, and then it turns out, you will be happy."

You see, our beliefs are simply thoughts that we keep thinking. When you learn that you have power and control over your thoughts, you can shift and change your entire established belief system, and instead carefully choose thoughts that serve and help you, rather than thoughts that negatively challenge and defeat you. When you begin to test this, and see how quickly your life and circumstances around you change, it can be fun, exciting, and sometimes a little scary. When you realize how much power you have over your own life and circumstances, it can be a tough idea to swallow, but so powerful when you do decide to embrace it.

I practiced the counselor's words of wisdom, and I made it through the entire year with this simple theory and practice. I spent every morning focusing on positive thoughts, and when negative thoughts came into my head throughout the day, I emotionally hugged them, released them, and then took the time and effort to focus on a better feeling thought that supported me. Sometimes our brains like to trick us into thinking that the thoughts we think are real. But in reality, you only have to own the thoughts that you want to, and you are free to let the negative ones go. How powerful and freeing is that? This changed everything I felt inside, and as a result, changed my reality. I used my thoughts to trick myself into being happy, and it actually worked. I then became determined to make big things happen for myself and my career, and I was so excited to wake up every day to simply live, experience, and play around with my newfound awareness.

The next year ended up being the best year of my life, and it continued to improve from there.

After realizing how much control my thoughts had over my life, I realized how powerful the Law of Attraction was. Law of Attraction is simply defined as, 'The Power of Positive Thinking.' All of the concepts in this book are based on this simple philosophy, and you will often hear me refer to The Law of Attraction later in the book.

Here is the recipe:

to happiness in a nutshell: (Positive Thoughts = Positive Feelings = Positive state of being) Write it down and remind yourself of this practice every day.

2. How to Become a Positive and Happy Person

"Happy looks good on you" - **Kristina Tsipouras**

She,

In the dark,

Found light

Brighter than many ever see.

She,

Within herself,

Found loveliness,

Through the souls own mastery.

And now the world receives

From her dower:

The message of the strength

Of inner power.

-Langston Hughes

Most of us were not taught at a young age that happiness is the key driver to a successful life. Many of us grew up being told that life is tough, that you have to work hard for your money, that college, graduate school, and the most demanding careers are the most important things to strive for. My father came to this country from Greece when he was twenty with only a hundred dollars in his pocket. He always focused on the traditions of our culture; good food, wine, family, friends, and health. He understood and instilled in us that being able to feel joy and happiness in everyday life is true success and abundance. Success isn't just about the money that you have in your bank account. He went on to open a dry cleaning business, bought two properties in an affluent town outside of Boston, retired early, and now spends summers in Greece, winters in Florida and the holidays with my sister and I in Boston. He is still the happiest person I know, and reminds me every time we speak, that "the most important thing is to be happy!" (Yes, he actually makes us say this out loud before we hang up the phone. As a teenager, I wanted to kill him for making me say this aloud, but now I look forward to it.)

If you didn't grow up with a father like mine, and were taught that life is supposed to be tough, I want you to challenge these theories. I want you to quit faster. I want happiness to be the key driver in your life. If your parents', friends', or society's ideas are not serving you, and are not giving you joy and happiness, then don't focus your time and energy on them.

3. The Recipe to Happiness

"Peace comes from within. Do not seek it without." - **Buddha**

I was once told that it is important to know whom you should listen to and why. Are you listening to people and taking advice from others who have what you want? Are you surrounding yourself with the right mentors and friends? As I took the plunge into entrepreneurship at the age of 26, I quit my nine to five career. I moved back to Boston, started waitressing at night to pay the bills, working on my company during the day, and moved home with my parents after living in my own apartment on the Upper East Side of Manhattan. Many people in my life were horrified! "Why would you take such a risk? Why would you leave such a fabulous career?" they said.

20

The advice above though came at the right time, and I started to pay attention to who's advice I was receiving, and then more importantly, who's advice I should take. Most of the negative advice came from those who work hard in their nine to five jobs, and who enjoy comfort and repetition. The positive and inspiring advice came from those who took similar risks, whose motivation surpassed their fears, and who lived the type of life that I wanted to live. So if your best friend, your professor, or someone in your life is offering you their opinion, make sure they have what you want before you listen to them or take it to heart. I would also follow this same advice in all areas of your life. Health, love, abundance, etc.

Now that you know who to listen to in order to build

the future you want, it is also a crucial step to find appreciation for how far you have come, and where you are in this very moment. When thinking about where you are today, and where you want to go tomorrow, it is important to radically accept your circumstances and embrace them. If you can't, it is going to be very hard for you to move forward. I practiced this by not focusing on envy, but instead on gratitude for my mentors who already had what I wanted. I converted my envy into inspiration to work hard on myself, and to become successful and happy as well. I have brought everything I wanted into my life this way, and I continue to do so by practicing these teachings each day. Remember, when envy or jealousy comes in, it is natural. But the most powerful tool you can give yourself is learning how to change your envy and jealousy into motivation and inspiration to move you forward. Often, I ask my mentors to tell me the stories about where they began. It keeps us real, human, and relatable. Many people started their first company in their basement and most of us had braces and acne in high school. We are all little ugly ducklings, our own worst critics, and it is all about overcoming the negative self talk and the limitations that our own fears and limiting beliefs put on us.

Two years ago, I was accepted into a startup competition created by the Founder of Under Armour, Kevin Plank. The name of the competition is called Cupid's Cup. After making it through to the top five out of thousands of candidates, Kevin Plank himself flew us out to the Under Armour headquarters in

Baltimore. He sat down with us and explained where the title Cupid's Cup came from. It all started with his first business, a rose delivery service that he started in his grandmother's basement while in college. He shared with us that success isn't about where you started and it isn't about where you are going. It isn't about the big wins along the way, it is about winning every single day. So what does winning mean to you? Is it about working hard at the office, spending quality time with friends and loved ones? Exercising and cooking nutritious meals for you and your family? Take the time to write out your priorities, and what success and happiness looks like for you in your daily life. This may be different for everyone, and we don't all value the same things. This is what makes the world go round, and it is okay to be different. It is time to

OWN being different. Bask in it, and go be your authentic self.

Happiness simplified:

We are picky about the clothes we wear, the colleges we attend, the career paths we choose, yet we're not nearly as picky about the thoughts we think. Our thoughts are what drive every choice that we make, and it is most important that we monitor our thoughts for our own wellbeing.

In this book, I'm going to ask you to become more selective with the thoughts that you think. I learned about the importance of this practice through studying the work of Jerry and Esther Hicks; I like to refer to them as the 'Godfathers of Law of Attraction.'

My friend and colleague Anna Tsui, a Boston life coach, shares what Law of Attraction is in five simple steps:

- What you believe shapes how you see the world.

- How you see the world influences how you react to the world.

- How you react to the world dictates what you do, how you behave, and what you create.

- What you create is what you get.

- What you get is a reflection of what you believe.

Find your bliss (Allowing vs. Resisting):

This chapter includes one of the most important tools that I can teach you. Before making decisions, plans, or anything else, ask yourself these questions: "Is it helping me? Is it serving me? Does it flow easily into my experience? Does it make me feel good, excited, and open?" If the answer is "no," then don't do it. Life is supposed to be easy and enjoyable. If it isn't, then you are most likely in resistance and pushing against something. Every day you should ask yourself this question, "Am I in resistance or am I in allowance?" Allowance means you are going with the flow. Resistance means you are trying to control a situation or outcome.

Letting go of the oars of life, and instead letting your feelings guide you and simply being open to everything that comes your way takes great courage and strength. But when you do, life will start to flow so much easier, and will soon become more enjoyable.

Now, I want you to understand one of the cornerstones of this new mindset. You have complete control over your circumstances and how you choose to define things. Nothing has meaning until you decide to give it meaning. This way of thinking is extremely powerful and can help us through the hardest times in our lives.

For instance, if you hate your current job, you can choose to define it as something that serves you and supports you, or you can choose to define it as something that is holding you back. Shift your perspective and definition of this current job, or any circumstance in your life. For example: "I know that my current position is allowing me an experience to better define what it is that I do want, and what makes me happy. I now have the motivation to define what it is that I do want in my next position, and I can use that motivation and clarity to begin my new job search. I am so excited for the future, and what is ahead of me. I know that the possibilities are endless, I just have to be open and positive to receive them."

Or, an example of resistance is this reaction: "I hate my job, how did I end up here? It isn't fair, what did I do to deserve this. Life is hard, and I am so over it."

The bottom line is that I want you to lighten up, and enjoy life a little more. Play, fail, get up, learn, and start again. It's fun if you allow it to be. #busygirltribe

Magical vs. practical thinking:

I grew up going to church on Christmas and Easter, but that was about it for my religious/spiritual upbringing. My Yia-Yia (Greek grandmother) would make me kneel at the end of my bed and pray with her every night when I spent summers with my family in Greece. We thanked God for giving us a beautiful day, good food to eat, and a healthy and happy loving family to spend time with. It always felt good to pray, to appreciate, and bless the good things in life. But I never connected with a God, and it is hard to wrap my mind around putting a name or picture on something that no one even knows for sure exists.

As I went on through life, and began my self-help journey, I did find and connect to spirituality. I believe that many forms of spirituality in addition to religion, are beautiful support systems honoring a community and a mindset that train us to be thankful, appreciative, and to always focus on the good. Both spirituality and religion support us throughout our lives; they are both beautiful things to connect to. We can enter meditation or mindfulness to feel that support and connection. Maybe it is our own soul, or our higher self, or the Universe, or a God that we connect to. The reality of this physical lifetime is that we all experience our own inner reality. We all experience life and daily circumstances differently from our neighbors. So whatever you want to believe, whatever supports you, follow it, pray to it, meditate on it. Do whatever you need to do in this life to feel supported, loved, and happy. You should not be ashamed honoring yourself, connecting to, and supporting your sensitive side. Many people go through life ignoring this side and as a result, life can feel like it is happening to you, rather than for you. That goes for this book as well and anything that you read. Take a few pieces away that you can relate to, and drop the rest. You don't need to understand or relate to every concept as different practices and beliefs work for different people.

Again, here is another example of allowing or resisting; Some people have very practical, factual, and scientific minds. They rationalize things this way, and often don't connect to any kind of spirituality (aka my boyfriend). When I talk to some of my friends about the Universe, sage, and Law of Attraction workshops, they often laugh and shake their heads, but they also support me in my beliefs. The point is that we don't have to all agree, we don't have to think the same, or believe what our friends, family, or even our significant others believe. What we do need is respect, appreciation, and freedom to think and believe the way we want to.

I have overcome some tough stuff in my life. From dealing with mental and alcohol abuse with close loved ones, to being dead broke with no clear path ahead, to feeling depressed and down, and overcoming anxiety and ADHD. I have experienced a lot, more than most should by my age. There is a reason why I turned to spirituality for support. There is a reason why I am happy, successful, and live a healthy balanced life today. There is a reason why I wake up feeling positive, motivated, and confident each day. And for that, I thank my supporting belief system (Law of Attraction) and spirituality. It is often the people who have gone through the toughest of times that end up finding the highest enlightenment, so do not feel badly about where you came from or what you have gone through, or are currently going through. Let these tough circumstances instead serve you and enlighten you.

Based on my experiences, I have grown to believe in a higher purpose and power. I do believe that in my life everything has happened for a reason, and that I am here for a specific purpose. For those who cannot get on board with magical thinking, try thinking practically about it. For example, it has been scientifically proven that the placebo pill actually works. If you believe that you are taking medicine curing an ailment that you have, the placebo often actually does cure the ailment. Of course, the opposite is also true. If you don't believe that the medication you are taking is working, then it is very likely that it won't work. Essentially, whatever you believe and feel will be your reality. It is as simple as that. I invite you to play in the world of positive thinking and spirituality and to always have an open mind. Whatever serves you and makes you feel supported and happy, that is what you should follow. Forget the rest, and make it about you and your journey. Honor what you need in your life. You are the only one who knows how to support yourself in the best way possible. It is also a part of life to play, test and figure it out along the way, so start playing a little more and stop taking yourself so seriously! A little sense of humor and some playfulness can go along way during tough times. So turn on comedy central or your favorite funny movie and just chill out if you need a break.

Getting into the vortex:

You know those days when you feel magical? Like everything is working for you? Life is beautiful, you feel like you are floating on clouds, and you are so happy that nothing can touch you? In Law of Attraction terms, we call this, The Vortex. The Vortex is a vibration and a state of being that happens when you are truly connected to your source (soul), your inner power and the real you. You are living honestly, happily, and everything is going your way. Everything you want is in The Vortex. When you are in this really happy state of being, get specific about what you want, and make it happen. If you want to understand the concept of the vortex in greater detail, search Abraham Hicks and The Vortex on YouTube. When you aren't feeling like yourself, you are down, or just low on energy, don't get specific about what you want. Don't focus on action or trying to figure it all out. Focus instead on what you can do to feel good in this very moment. Call a friend, take a walk, browse an uplifting website. Just don't try to get too specific about anything when you aren't in The Vortex (your happy place) or feeling good. Again, the easiest way to create "a good mood" is to create more general thoughts. So turn on a funny show, cook a yummy dish, just shut your mind off and relax for a moment. Work on making intentions, not goals. Intentions have a softer vibration than goals, so they tend to feel more approachable, light, easy and enjoyable.

How to change your reality:

Everything you want in life is already within you. Really, this sounds so cliché, but it is true. For instance, you can be in a very unhealthy, dependent relationship. Maybe you have given power to someone else, and you have allowed that person to have control over your feelings. But guess what? YOU have the power to take that control back, and to shift your reality quickly. When you do, they won't know what hit them and why their reactions no longer affect you. It is a really powerful tool when you learn how to use it. I used this when I was in college to get out of an unhealthy and dependent relationship, and it was so empowering.

All of a sudden, I took my happiness into my own hands and no longer leaned on my long distant boyfriend to fill me up since he wasn't doing a very good job at it anyways! I started going to the gym every day, joining extra curriculars, putting myself out there to make friends, and even just enjoyed walking around campus and filling myself up with appreciate and love for the simple things that I experienced every day. For example, the sun shining, my Professor acknowledging my idea in class, re-decorating my mood board on my wall, etc.

As soon as I started to care less, called less often and focused on my own life and being present each day, he started calling more and becoming more available to me. I ended the relationship in the end because it wasn't healthy and I soon realized that I actually didn't need him or want to anymore. You see, any circumstance in your life can change so quickly, because you and your thoughts have ultimate control over every situation no matter how stuck you currently feel in it. Often, people look to the outside world to fix things or control situations. It is easy to blame other people for your current situation, but this will only leave you stuck. I want you to instead go inside yourself, because you don't have power over anything outside you and your own reality. What you do have power over though, is to define and change your thoughts around any situation. This, in turn, will change your physical reality as well.

Realize that there is a shift that you need to make inside yourself to change your physical reality or circumstances. For example, start with writing a letter to the Universe, demanding back your control and power. Focus on loving yourself, and lifting yourself up every day. Remind yourself that no one has power or control over you. Realize that your reality, and the people in your life, are having their own experiences, and they only show up in your life as mirrors of how you feel about yourself on the inside. When you respect yourself and love yourself more, people who respect and love you will start showing up in your life too. If you have a lack of respect and self-love, then people in your life will also have a lack of respect and love for you. So practice going inward and loving yourself first, not the other way around.

If you are in a relationship where someone may be taking advantage of you, and not treating you with the respect that you deserve, ask yourself this question: "Do I truly love and respect myself? Do I demand respect from others? Do I care if others respect me? Do I care what others think of me?" Then, work on shifting your definition of yourself, the situation, and the experience you are having. For starters, write a list of everything that you love about yourself, the value you have, and what you give to others. Write your Busy Girl contract and make this shift your priority. Put yourself first! Let working out, eating healthy, and making a five-year plan with personal and professional goals an important part of your life, and take back your control. Make it about you, enjoy being selfish, make the shift, and watch how attractive you will become to the outside world.

People today can feel vibrations and authenticity so deeply. You know that feeling when someone walks into the room and you just feel their presence? They are warm and glowing, their smile lights up the room and you just want to be around them? That is someone who has mastered their own reality. They live for themselves and their own internal experience. Because they put themselves first, they have so much to offer the world, and to others. These types of shifts and experiences happen all the time, and they are so beautiful to watch. Just take the tools from this book, and start there. Enjoy this experience and shift, make it fun, and when you find your own power within you, kick that controlling partner or friend to the curb!

Forgiveness:

Ah, forgiveness, A beautiful thing! Forgiveness can be freeing, empowering, and brings you great comfort and joy. Only strong people are capable of forgiveness. People who are free, those are the ones who know how to forgive and move on. Here are five simple tools to practice forgiveness:

- **Forgive yourself** (mentally or write it down) - Remember that you are doing the best that you can with the tools that you have, and that is all that this world asks of you. You don't owe any larger explanation to yourself or anyone else. If that doesn't feel good to you, go a little deeper and explain why you are forgiving yourself.

- **Forgive the other person** (mentally or write it down) - Remember that they too, are doing the best that they can with the tools that they have. Everyone is on their own journey. The only power you have is how you define the situation and how you decide to overcome it. (Later in the book we will explain soul types.

This will help you better understand the difficult people that show up in your life.)

- **Write down what you took away from the situation** What did you learn? How did this person serve as a teacher giving you beautiful gifts of wisdom and hard lessons learned? Remember that life and every scenario that occurs is happening for you and not to you. It is all about perspective and rising above. This is the attitude that most happy and successful people have and practice every day.

- **How will you do it differently next time?** Did you feel good about yourself and did you handle the situation with ease and grace? What could you do better next time? What would make you feel better about yourself and the situation that occurred? Are you being true to yourself and honoring YOUR needs first?

I have practiced these steps of forgiveness time and time again. It is a powerful practice that releases and heals us all. In the past, I would often get stuck in the guilt trip phase. That fiery Greek pride came out, and I held onto anger, not letting go or forgiving and releasing the other person from my thoughts. And you know where that got me? Nowhere! This often happened as a teenager when I would fight with my parents, if a friend betrayed me, if a boyfriend didn't rise up to my expectations, and in business partnerships as well.

You see though, when you forgive and release a

person or situation from your life, you are going with the flow (letting go of the oars). You are in allowance and not resistance. When you move with this flow of life, the Universe will begin to open new doors and opportunities for you. But when you are stuck in the past and are holding onto something, the only person who is going to stay stuck is you. Often, conflict arises for good reason. It is the Universe's way of saying, "Ok Kristina, it is time to move on." We've got a better guy waiting for you, let's ditch this one already. He had to cheat on you because you weren't going to let him go any other way! You are welcome, that was a gift for you to move onward and upward!" The same goes with friends, colleagues, and sometimes family members as well. If you aren't vibrating at the same frequency as others, conflict will often arise and that is your sign to move on, because bigger and better things are waiting for you just around the corner. All you have to do is forgive, let go, and move on. I like to define 'letting go' of things as not 'letting go', but instead letting it grow. Letting it grow means saying goodbye to something because it is preventing you from growing into a better person. It is not just time to not move away from that thing that is holding you back, but more importantly move closer to the person you are supposed to be. It is a beautiful way to peacefully and positively say goodbye and move on. Now say it with me...." don't let it go, let it grow!"

4. S.E.N. The 3 Most Important Tools According to Happy People

"The greatest wealth is health." - **Virgil Latin**

Every successful Busy Girl must become a master of health and balance. There are three simple priorities that we often overlook, but they affect every single decision that we make.

S.E.N. stands for Sleep, Exercise, and Nutrition and are the three top priorities in order to achieve daily bliss and happiness.

Again, when setting your health goals, or any goals in life, focus on setting intentions instead of goals. Intentions have a softer vibration than goals. So they tend to feel more approachable, light, easy and enjoyable. It is better to set intentions when changing

50

your habit or lifestyle. We are human, we might get off track, and that is ok. Just be aware of it, and jump right back on! This will keep the mindset, on focusing on happiness and not overwhelm you.

Start here: Keep track of daily healthy habits and note how you feel each day. I created a daily planner (The Busy Girl planner) that helps track these three priorities, in addition to focusing on the balance of personal and professional goals and intentions. Go to busygirldaily.com to find the busy girl planner to help keep you on track and make the journey more enjoyable. Or go to Paper Source, The Container Store, Bed Bath & Beyond or other stores that sell daily planners.

1. **Sleep:** Did I get enough sleep last night?

2. **Nutrition:** Do I feel good about what I ate yesterday?

3. **Exercise:** Did I exercise?

These three things need to become your top priority. In other words, you need to become your top priority. When you are working out at least three days a week, eating healthy and getting the proper amount of sleep each night, your mood, energy, creativity, productivity level, and absolutely everything around you will improve.

When I began to live a healthier lifestyle, everything changed for me. I am more focused, ideas and opportunities flow more easily to me, and I accomplish more, faster. I am happier, I have more energy, inspiration, and overall, I am more fulfilled and satisfied in my everyday life. Routine is very healthy for us as humans. Just like a child is nurtured by a routine and schedule, we are the same way as adults. I want you to keep a journal and track your sleep, food and exercise every week. Find a planner like the Busy Girl Planner, or one that tracks these priorities for you.

Everyone is different, but here is an example of my daily journal and needs. Apps like Wunderlist or Evernote are also amazing tools for keeping check-lists, positive aspects lists, daily journals and more!

Sleep:

9 hours (11 p.m. - 8 a.m.)

(Yes, I need a lot of sleep, and I own that. Work on radically accepting your needs. Everyone is different!)

Exercise:

30 minutes to walk or jog on the treadmill

30 minutes weights, abs, yoga, and stretch

Nutrition:

Breakfast: Berry, banana, kale and perfect fit protein shake.

Lunch: Leftover chicken stir-fry

Dinner: Grilled salmon and asparagus

Snack: Chocolate-covered edamame and turmeric tea

When you start focusing on **S.E.N.**, you won't only look and feel better, you will start building the self-esteem you need to be a successful busy girl. When you make healthy choices and habits for yourself, you are telling yourself, "I am worth it." I cannot urge you enough to take these three habits seriously and track them each week. They will change your life. While doing so, have fun with it! Experiment with new food, take a crazy exercise dance class, and don't kill yourself over a piece of cake, or bag of Stacy's pita chips (my weakness).

Some easy tips to live by:

- Sunday and Monday are the most important days of the week. They set the tone for the entire week ahead. Work on making these days productive and healthy and the rest of the week should fall into place.

- Make Saturday or Sunday YOUR day! (Cook, clean, prepare for the week ahead, and play a little. Practice saying "no" and making YOU your first priority at least one day a week.)

- Never miss a Monday workout, ever.

- Get in three days a week of exercise. No more white carbs, stick to whole wheat/whole grain.

- Eat a cupcake and enjoy it once in a while. Don't deprive yourself of anything.

- Sleep in and enjoy it. Wake up slowly on the weekends... and the weekdays, if you have the luxury

BUSY GIRL ACTIVITY 2

Appreciation List

This activity is simple and very powerful. Each day, write a list of three things that you appreciate. It can be as simple as:

1. The beautiful blue sky.

2. A fridge full of delicious food to cook with.

3. An email from an old colleague.

Add to this list each day. Keep it by your bed, in the notes section of your phone, on wunderlist, evernote or in a journal. This activity helps us to appreciate and honor the little things in life and the everyday joys. When looking back to a month's long appreciation list, I feel so much joy and happiness when I read it back to myself. This daily practices keeps us in the appreciation state of mind which is a very powerful place to be.

PART 2

How to Thrive

Don't just survive, learn to Thrive! **- Arianna Huffington**

1. Face Your Fears

F.E.A.R. *"False Evidence Appearing Real"* - ***Unknown***

When you face anything in your life head on, it gets resolved quicker and eventually disappears. The same goes with fear. A simple tool that will instantly make you feel better about a situation that bothers you is this:

On the top of a piece of paper, write down your fear. Below it, take the fear and go down the path of what could happen. For example:

My Fear: Losing my job:

Step 1. I would not be able to pay my bills.

Step 2. I would have to move in with my mom or my friend.

Step 3. I would update my resume.

Step 4. I would start to think of new areas of work that I have never considered before.

Step 5. I would volunteer at a local shelter and put life into perspective.

Step 6. I would realize and tell myself each day that this situation is only temporary.

Step 7. I would pick up some part-time work at a gym and get a free membership.

Step 8. I would become physically and mentally fit.

Step 9. I would spend evenings networking, and would reach out to everyone in my network for job opportunities.

Step 10. I would eventually find a job again, and be stronger and better for going through this situation.

You can do this for each fear in life that you have. When you face your fears head on, they are not as scary as when they are hidden in the back of your mind. Avoidance can be much scarier than sitting down and facing your fears. When doing this, make sure that you have a support system around you. Friends, family, co-workers, and if you don't feel comfortable facing your fears in front of someone else, become your own support system. Tell yourself that everything is going to be ok. More than ok, everything is going to be better, it is going to be great!

2. **Confidence and Self-Esteem**

"I say if I'm beautiful, I say if I'm strong. You will not determine my story." - **Amy Schumer**

It took me until the age of 29 to value my self-worth. I have never spoken publicly about this subject, but I feel confident enough now to share my story. As a teenager, I developed early, and have received a lot of male attention my entire life, yet; I have always struggled with my self-worth and value. I felt safe dating people who loved me more than I loved them, and stayed in relationships too long because of this. I actually defined a lot of my self-worth on the attention that I received. Growing up, society put so much emphasis on size, looks, and perfection. Young people today gain so much false self-esteem by being praised for shallow compliments based on looks and attractiveness. Does this do anything for their soul? Does it help self-value, worth, and confidence? I believe the answer is no. Some of the most attractive people I have ever come across in my life actually have the lowest self-esteem. There is a missing link here that society tends to overlook.

I, personally, have always considered myself attractive. I have always loved my body, but I could always be better, I could always look a little more perfect. I never felt satisfied, and continued to be hard on myself. I still today struggle with perfectionism, but I have taken control of many areas of my life, and one is knowing my self-worth and value, and never letting a man or anyone else define that for me.

At the age of 28, I broke a pattern. This pattern was letting men into my life who were simply not good for me. I became picky for the first time, and didn't just jump at male attention. When I was dating, even when I felt a connection, got excited, went on a few dates, and it turns out that it just wasn't going to work out, I simply said, "on to the next!" And there is always a next. The truth of the matter is, when you value yourself, your worth and your time, you simply stop having time for people who aren't a perfect match, or for anyone who treats you any less than you deserve.

To create this shift in my life, and to not let anyone, especially a man, determine my self-worth and happiness, is the most brilliant gift I have ever received. It takes time to get there, it takes practice and tools (many that are in this book), but I tell you, no matter who you are, no matter what you look like, you can get there. Could you imagine life if you decided to never let another person determine your happiness or self-worth? What if you had full control over it, no matter what life brings? This, my friends, is enlightenment, and it is strong. Once it is learned, it cannot be undone. Sure, I still have moments of weakness, but these moments only last a few minutes, a few hours at most. But soon after, they shift into brilliant lessons, courage and strength to move forward, and to keep the focus on me.

Begin here: Value and accept rejection. It is such a valuable part of the process, and a blessing, if you let it be. Rejection, on their end or on yours, is honestly just two souls that are not a perfect match or simply just bad timing. Nothing more, nothing less. I challenge you to redefine your own meaning of rejection, and what it truly means to you. Give it a purpose, give it value and you will never let the disappointment be greater than the lesson. An example of rejection that I re-defined in my own life was when I applied for my dream job at 25. I went through five rounds of interviews and then got rejected, hard. I was such a perfect fit; I had all the qualifications, yet they didn't want me. I never wanted something so bad, and I never understood why they didn't accept me. Six years later though, I realized that that perfect job would have limited my next career move and would have stalled my own happiness, my move to NYC, starting my first company and wouldn't have been the right fit for me after all. It simply wasn't meant to be and the Universe had much greater plans for me. The Founder of that company who had rejected me actually just recently reached out to ask if they could speak at my business women's conference! Now I laugh at the past and appreciate those doors that never opened. So in the moment, try to accept rejection and realize that there is a deeper meaning and purpose behind why it didn't work out. Some day you will see it, so for now laugh, keep smiling, stay open and move forward.

Now back to the type of rejection that hurts the worst. If you were recently rejected by someone you were interested in, begin here: Write a letter to the Universe talking about your future boyfriend or girlfriend and how amazing they are. How do they treat you? How do they make you feel? What qualities do you love about them? What type of life have you built together? Read it back to yourself often, and wait for that perfect partner. Don't settle for anything less. Wait for your best friend; the person who is capable of pushing you to be a better person, just as you hope to do the same for them. The person who has taken time to work on themselves, and not settle for anything less than an amazing life and happily ever after. No matter what age you are, if you have not yet found your life partner, do not get frustrated. You are exactly where you are supposed to be. After all, the happiest couples that I have come across actually met later in life, when they were fully developed into the person they wanted to be. They conquered the world, solo. From that, they learned valuable lessons that only change you, when you allow yourself to be vulnerable. The most enlightened people in this world have seen some of the darkest times so enjoy the journey to finding the one.

Always look towards the light, and know that you deserve the most amazing relationship and you'll be happy ever after one day. The opportunity will come when the timing is right. Please let go, trust the process, settle down and have some fun along the way!

3. How to Quickly Overcome Heartbreak & Loss:

"Everything lost, is found again, in a new form in a new way.

Everything hurt is healed again, in a new life, in a new day."

- **Unknown**

Heartbreak and mourning the loss of someone, no matter who it was, or what the situation is can be a difficult, confusing, and a frustrating process that has many ebbs, flows, ups and downs. It is a very emotional experience that requires a lot of patience, but most importantly, it requires being good to yourself.

You have to decide what is right for you, but having some sort of closure is usually important. You are ending a chapter in your life, and opening the door to a new one. Sometimes it isn't a happy ending, which is usually why you are moving on.

Wait until you are in a good and happy mental state with lots of support around you. Warn friends and family that you will need their support throughout this time.

When you are in a place that feels good, or 'the vortex,' it won't be a feeling of moving away from someone, it will be a 'coming home' feeling closer to yourself and finding the right partner for you. You might feel a great sense of sadness, and at the same time, a great sense of relief. It will feel like you are allowing, not resisting the natural flow of your life that is supposed to always feel good. You may be feeling some heartbreak and relief at this time, or it may come

72

in waves. This is natural.

Practice this belief system; everything happening in my life is happening for me, not to me. It is bringing me closer to happiness and success. Difficult situations and people in my life are only here to serve me and teach me valuable lessons in order to reach my fullest potential. I am thankful for them, I appreciate them, I bless them. I release them, I heal them, and I let them go.

Often, we fall in love with the idea of a person. We actually love the idea of them more than we love their presence. Take everything that this person has showed you about what you do not want in a partner, and instead write a story of what you do want (similar to the positive contrast list above, but in letter form to the Universe). You see, in order to find out what you do want, you have to go through what you don't want. So every time you find a partner who doesn't love you enough, who isn't successful enough, who doesn't connect with you the way you desire, it simply creates the desire and opportunity for a better partner to come in. Again, I literally want you to write a letter to the Universe, asking for the type of partner you want. Or even better, write a story as if you already found that partner, and be descriptive about how he or she makes you feel and how happy you are. The point is to try to shift your mind to feel these thoughts before you create them in your life. I did this, and couldn't believe when that partner, who met all of those needs showed up in my life. It was only when I was complete and whole that I attracted someone who was complete and whole as well.

Example love letter to the Universe:

Dear Universe,

I feel so fortunate to have met the man of my dreams. He is the most caring, loving and amazing partner that I have ever been with. He respects and understands me on a deeper level than I have ever felt before. He is funny, kind, intelligent, respectful, handsome and successful. He is driven and in love with life. He feels like my best friend, and I couldn't imagine going through life with anyone else.

Trick your mind into feeling that you have already met this person, or are about to meet them. Stay in excitement mode to move forward quickly. Trick your mind into thinking that you already have this. Practice how you would feel if this person was in your life. Write it down, and read the story to yourself every night!

Here are some things to focus on while going through this tough time:

1. Be good to yourself (shopping, spa, dinner with friends, etc.). If you are on a budget, watch funny movies, make dinner at home, scrapbook, create, spend time in nature, etc.

2. Watch movies and cry, mourn the relationship, it is a healthy step. Just don't get stuck here for more than a few days or a week, tops.

3. Get healthy. When you put your healthy diet,

workout schedule and routine as the first priority in your life, it will be hard to stay down or in a negative place.

4.   If you get stuck in limbo, example: the makeup/breakup scenario, make a list of the cons of this person and why you are trying to get away from them. Is this the love story you want to be telling your children about one day? You deserve a beautiful love story and a beautiful life.

5. The day you break up, make a reservation at your favorite restaurant. You can only keep the reservation if you stay true to your goal, which is not talking/texting/ranting on social media/staying true to yourself for one month. After a month, buy yourself a present. Maybe tell your best friend and family, and they will chip in too! At month two, maybe even a

weekend getaway? Have fun with it! You will be so proud of yourself and feel so good when you hit these goals. Share with your fellow busy girls so that we can support you and help keep you on track using this hashtag! #busygirltribe

6.   Search deep inside for the power within you. Find your inner strength. Empower yourself. Do nice things for others, make an appreciation list of what you admire in yourself. Make a list of things you want in your future relationship, write a story to the Universe about the person you want to be with.

7.   Eventually find a place to feel positive about your past. Bless the relationship and that person for teaching you many things, and taking you a step closer to the relationship that is right for you.

8.   Remind yourself that you have to go through negative relationships to learn more about yourself and what you want and deserve for your next relationship.

(A friend once told me, it's wrong until it's right. And in love, it really is that simple; with "the one" it will feel easy, almost effortless.)

9. Trust me, he/she is out there looking as hard for you as you are for him/her.

10. Work on being the perfect partner, rather than working on finding the perfect partner.

11. It is ok to continue to love someone who wasn't right for you, even from afar. Don't beat yourself up if they stay in your thoughts, even years later when you are in a happy new relationship. It is normal, and as soon as you accept this, you won't think of them as

often.

Here are a few daily practices that will help you begin to build your confidence:

- Make a list of what you have accomplished so far in life and what you have overcome

- Make a list of what you are proud of

- Make a list of what you love about yourself

- Get your hair and make-up done, dress up and get professional photos taken.

- Remember when looking in a mirror that mirrors are two-dimensional. You will never be able to experience and feel how others see and experience you. Beauty and attraction is a vibration inside that everyone is capable of carrying. Attraction is directly linked to confidence and only you can define how attractive you come off when entering a room.

- Focus on daily meditation and listen to the Orin and DaBen meditations on self-confidence and beauty. Practice the meditations that fill up your heart and soul with bright white light. https://www.orindaben.com/catalog/singles_dow nloads/

- Make S.E.N. your top 3 priorities and watch your confidence and self-love grow each day that you treat your body right.

4. Turning Negative into Positive

"Someday, everything will make perfect sense. So for now, laugh at the confusion, smile through tears, and keep reminding yourself that everything happens for a reason."

- Paulo Coelho

Your happiness isn't in someone else's control; it is in yours!

These tools become so powerful, that after some time, you are going to be blessing the person who broke your heart, the friend that betrayed you, the boss that fired you, and the person that cut you off while driving and caused you to wreck your car. You see, in the theory of Law of Attraction, we believe that everything happens for a reason and that you are in control of your life and circumstances. When something negative shows up, it has great purpose, power, and meaning.

Do those old negative patterns keep coming back? Is it because you still have something to learn from the situation that keeps coming into your life? Nothing will go away until we have taken the lesson away from it that we were meant to learn. You see, everyone in your life, every conversation, every confrontation, is simply a mirror of exactly how you feel on the inside. If you feel confident and powerful, you will get the job. If you feel fearful and insecure, you will not get the job. If you feel worthy of true love, you will receive it. If you do not, you will be betrayed time and time again with different partners. I want you to now look at the negatives in your life, instead as the positives. It is time to redefine negativity, and let these instances serve you instead of defeat you. For it is because of these negative experiences that you become the strongest, the wisest, and the bravest. It is while going through these difficult experiences where you will learn, grow, and develop the seeds of your confidence and self-worth. Each and every negative situation has so much power and meaning that you can learn to truly be thankful for them. Every day, you get to choose. You get to define everything in your life. Remember, that no one has power over you. Nothing has meaning, until you define it. You can choose to take any situation and make it positive, or negative.

It is also important in life, to see and experience what you do not want, in order to understand what you do want. In Law of Attraction terms, we call this "launching rockets of desire." For example: "My old car broke down, I really hate that stupid old car!" This experience gives you the tools you need (maybe frustration or determination) to sit back and figure out what it is that you do want. But if you didn't have the old car, if you didn't get frustrated, you wouldn't be able to define exactly what it is that you do want. So instead, I want you to try to list what is currently in your life that you do not want. From there, I want you to create a separate list, on another piece of paper that is the contrast to every item on your first list, the outcome of what you do want, based on your list of "don't wants." For example, on my first list I wrote: I feel lonely. Then on my second list, I wrote, I have a great group of loving and supportive friends.

After you are done, I want you to tear up, or burn the "don't wants" list. In order to focus on good-feeling thoughts, thoughts that support you, we need to start talking and thinking differently.

So instead of saying I really don't want that old car anymore (negative thought), instead say and think, "I love the idea of sitting in my brand new car" (positive thought). Have fun going a little deeper with it: "My new car would make me feel powerful, excited, and free! It would take me anywhere I wanted to go. I love how it smells, how the leather seats feel, I am so lucky to have a new car!" The point of this exercise is not to get frustrated, but to appreciate and accept where you are. Then get into the feeling of already having something before you have it. If this feels confusing to you, go easy on yourself. It took me about a year to shift my thinking and how I talk about my current circumstances. Search Abraham Hicks and appreciation or positive thinking on YouTube to learn more.

So now that you have learned some of the tools on how to shift from negative to positive, here is a re-cap of daily practices that can remind you how to continue to rise above and find happiness and positivity in every day:

1.   Eat clean (learn to cook simple, easy, and quick meals)

2.   Clean and declutter your home, your office, your surroundings

3.   Exercise (at least 3 days a week)

4.   Sleep/take naps

5.   Limit alcohol

6.   Healthy hygiene (blow dry your hair, put on makeup, wear clothes that make you feel good.

7.   Positive aspect list (Busy Girl Activity 1

8.   Appreciation list

9.   Letter to the Universe

9. Meditate

10. Happiness rituals

11. Essential oils

12. Deprivation tank

13. Vision board

14. Support system

15. Life anchors

(You will learn more about these practices later in the book)

5. Shifting Your Mood and Emotions

"Don't promise when you're happy. Don't reply when you're angry and don't decide when you're sad." - **Unknown**

Your emotions are meant to come in and out like waves in the ocean. You have to learn how to ride the waves, not let them knock you over. They are only temporary. When a negative emotion comes in, embrace it, heal it and release it back out to sea. Know that when you feel negative, it simply means that you are thinking about something that doesn't support you. This is simply part of the human condition. It is only when we hold onto negative thoughts and don't let them go that we get into a sticky situation or a negative behavior pattern. Remember, a bad feeling is simply a false belief. If you feel badly about what you are

89

thinking, it is because it is not true to who you are, it doesn't serve you, and it isn't yours to keep. So drop the thought, and challenge yourself to find a better thought/feeling around this situation that supports you and feels good.

Take control of your thoughts:

Begin every day with a ritual that serves you. Tell yourself that today you will have an amazing day. If your day starts to go the other way, then simply go neutral. Going neutral, and finding a good feeling thought now is the most important thing you can do for yourself. Feeling good and following positive thoughts, feelings, and experiences is how you will thrive and not just survive in life. Did your day honestly just suck? If so, then just let it go. Go neutral.

Be good to yourself and don't think about the particular situation or person bothering you until you are in a better place to deal with it. For now, put on a feel good movie, make your favorite dinner and be good to yourself. When you are in a more elevated state, after a good night's sleep, or after an evening with friends, then you can try to tackle the situation head on.

Going neutral can be very simple and basic. Focus on a simple feel good thought, like warm cookies out of the oven, your pet, the sun on your face, or a beautiful calm lake. Focus on a thought that makes you happy and automatically elevates your mood. One thing I do to quickly elevate my mood is making an online vision board using Pinterest. I have a private board titled, 'five-year plan' and I changed the automatic 'dream house' board title into my 'future house' board title because that title felt better and more exciting, even achievable! I enjoy adding to them, browsing pictures of pretty things, and it instantly elevates my mood. Websites like cuteoverload.com, or just searching YouTube for cute animal videos also does the trick!

Excitement:

The feeling of excitement is the most powerful tool in creating your future. It's important to feel excitement and appreciation for today, for how far you have come, and for everything that is waiting for you in the future! There is a beautiful balance of appreciating what you currently have, but leaving room for excitement for the future.

Pattern/Life interrupt:

Sometimes, the only way to get out of a funk is to create a pattern or life interrupt. My spiritual mentor, Asha, reminded me of this when I was feeling stuck. For me, this would always mean getting away. I would go to NYC and visit my girlfriends. We would laugh, drink, dance, play, find new inspiration and meet interesting people. This would always fill up my love and appreciation tank. When I returned home, I always had a new perspective and it allowed me to shift out of my funk. If you do not have the means to get away for the weekend, simply take a new route to work, go to a new place for lunch, take a new community class that you have never taken before, or buy something new at the grocery store that you have never tried before. It can be as small or as big as you want! Do something different, out of the norm that will create a shift and an interrupt in your current daily pattern.

Daily Rituals/Practice:

Create a sacred place in your home to be silent, meditate, reflect, journal, etc. Create a morning and evening ritual. For example, wake up, lay in bed for five minutes and do deep belly breathing. Do five minutes of yoga and stretching. Make a green smoothie and make an appreciation list. Focus on strengthening your core; breathe into this area when meditating, when speaking, etc. This is where women receive their inner strength and confidence; it is the lower part of your belly, under your belly button.

BUSY GIRL ACTIVITY 2

Life Anchors

In a journal, on a piece of paper that you can hang on the wall, or simply on your desktop, write out what your life anchors are. There are many areas that you can have a life anchor in. Life anchors are sort of like a bandage. They help you feel better and protect you immediately. They give you space and comfort to begin to let you heal, or simply change the tone of a day that may have started out negatively. Let's first list out what they are.

Friend to call: Jessa.

Family member to call: Mom.

Song: DJ, You've got my Love.

Outfit: Favorite grey long sleeve, Lulu lemon leggings, sneakers, ponytail & lip-gloss.

Food: Cheddar cheese & apple slices.

Drink: Iced Mint Chamomile with local honey.

Exercise: Sprinting 1 minute on 1 minute off 6 reps.

Hobby: Photography.

Distraction: Sex and The City episode.

Hobby 2: Browse Pinterest & create a vision board.

Setting: My favorite chair, pumpkin spice latte and calming music.

Book: Busy Girl's Guide to Happiness.

Mantra: I am worthy. I am worthy. I am worthy.

Scent: Lavender.

Now, I want you to take time to write down what your life anchors are; be as specific as you want, and know that this is your go-to list when you need support, to get out of your funk, or simply turn a bad day into a good one. Print it out and put it in your purse or on your bedside table. Let it be easily available to you. Let this list be your anchor and support system. It is healing to write out what supports you and to learn more about how to support yourself in a tough time. This activity is about creating your own rituals and customizing comfort that works specifically for you and your needs! You can go much deeper than what I have listed above.

PART 3

Money and creating abundance

"There's a certain delusional quality that all successful people have to have. You have to believe that something different will happen." - **Will Smith**

1. Show Me The Money!

"There are two kinds of people in this world. People who have money and people who are rich."

– Coco Chanel

If you hide from your money situation, then money will hide from you. You have to face your fears about money, and look at your debt, bills, and reality head on. Go through the 'face your fears' ritual that I shared with you earlier in the book; start by only working on this when you are in a good mood. Go ahead and play your favorite tunes, light a candle, pour a glass of your favorite red wine and put cookies in the oven. Also plan on a small or big reward afterward, like meeting with a friend to go on a walk, or watching your favorite movie. Reward yourself, because you deserve it. Dealing with money, and facing your fears can be difficult, but there are so many amazing resources out there today to help you. You aren't alone, and so many women are going through the same debt, bills, and money worries as you are today. #busygirltribe

Money is paper, it is simple and light; you have to be simple to receive it. Expansion and growth equals wealth, so never put limits on yourself or fall in love with one idea of how it is supposed to be. Stay curious and hungry, always growing and expanding.

If any part of your life feels stuck, your money will be stuck too. Stick to the tools that you have learned from this book:

- Face your fears (and write out the fear list).
- Are you in resistance and or allowance? (try to shift your thought process around money beliefs).
- Be open.
- Meditate.
- Vision board.

Shift your fears about money to love and appreciation. You must have a deep-felt love and appreciation for money to receive it. You have to work on your money relationship just like any other relationship in your life for it to grow, expand and get better and stronger! Do not ever doubt or question what you want. The world is full of abundance and success, and there is plenty of room at the top for you.

Who do you listen to? Talk to mentors who have what you want, who have saved, have been successful, and have made good investments. Try to find a money and success mentor and start planning monthly meetings and check-ins. Have an accountability partner, whatever works for you. There are many money coaches out there today to work with, but make sure you do your research first.

Get into the feeling of what it would feel like to have endless amounts of money, or enough to feel comfortable and be worry free. If you woke up every morning with lots of money and the freedom to do what you want with it, what would your day look like? Write out a story of your day. How would you feel emotionally, what would it bring up for you? What would you do? Who would you spend it with? Read this story to yourself every day and trick yourself into feeling like you already have it, like you are already successful. This will attract success and abundance into your life quickly.

What are your current beliefs about money and spending? If they are negative, feelings of guilt, shame, etc., make a list and tear it up or burn it if you have to.

Accept that these old belief systems no longer serve you. It is time to tell a new story, and write a new chapter. The beauty of the world that we live in today is that you can literally choose to wake up each morning and hit the re-set button. You can start fresh, change your beliefs and patterns and re-invent yourself. Make a new list about all the positive feelings you have about money, and focus on this list instead. When letting go of an old negative pattern and belief system, you have to radically embrace and accept it, thank it for its purpose in your life, and let it go. Visually, you can take these negative thoughts, put them in a balloon, let go of the string, and watch them drift away. You can also physically write them down, say "goodbye" to them, rip up the paper, and burn it. This is a very cleansing ritual that you can make your own.

In general, nothing has meaning until you give meaning to it. You have control over your definitions of money, success, happiness, health, etc. You can take any scenario in your current life, and change the definition of it in order to serve you better. For instance, say you are struggling financially and cannot see more than a month ahead. Instead of defining this as scary, you can define it as exciting. You can say to yourself, "I am a student of finance and I am learning more every month about how to become financially fearless. There are so many amazing free tools and resources around me, and I can see a very abundant future ahead." Start telling yourself a different story about your current situation, and start to see the struggle turn into an opportunity. You personally have the power to change any circumstance in your life, by simply starting to change your thoughts and belief system. Being aware and honoring your current situation is the first step!

What is valuable to you does not have to be valuable to everyone. Where did judgment come from anyway? Judging yourself, judging others, it comes from a place of fear. So if anyone is judging you or if you are judging yourself, simply send the people or yourself love. Appreciate the concern, but also recognize that it stems from their own fear and actually has nothing to do with you. If it feels good to you and you are in a state of excitement and allowing, then simply send them love and try to quiet them. However, if something they are saying triggers you deep inside, then they may be mirroring how you feel on the inside and may be showing up in your life to teach you a lesson. For example, about five years ago I was given the opportunity to become the lifestyle editor of a Facebook page, (Boston, Massachusetts). When I started, we only had 10,000 fans. I ended up becoming the only editor on the page and posted on it about three times a day. I engaged others and started to see the group grow very quickly. Three years later, I had built the group to over 350,000 fans. I discovered a great company, teespring.com where you could design and order shirts at no cost. I started to sell Boston themed shirts on the page and starting making a lot of money. It was flowing into my life easily and effortlessly and it started to feel too good to be true. I started becoming anxious and feeling guilty about how easy it was for me to make money. I also didn't feel that I had what it took to start my own page, so I spent three years building a public community page up for someone else. He soon realized the amazing opportunity that I had created for him and took over the page and removed me as an editor. I had a few times in my career that I made a lot of money, built up a successful business, but because of my own limiting beliefs in myself, they were taken away from me. Finally after being burnt a few times, I worked on my own self-worth and value and would never let someone take an opportunity or idea away from me again. Many of these lessons we do have to learn on our own and experience first-hand, but hopefully some of the stories in this book will make you think before you act and protect yourself before you get burnt too badly.

So remember, if you hide from your money situation and ignore your current reality, self-worth, self-esteem or any area in your life, than money will also hide from you. No matter where you are, you have to acknowledge, accept and value your current situation. Take it one step at a time. Start with baby steps if you have to.

I personally love having money dates. Make a date or money appointment every week, and make it enjoyable. Bake up a batch of cookies, open your favorite bottle of wine, buy a pretty organizer to get you excited, and start focusing on organizing bill pay, setting goals, seasonal budgets, etc. Do this every week, and get specific about your goals and intentions.

Write out the numbers and goals and set dates. These types of specifics give you knowledge, which in return give you power and confidence. How many books do I need to sell to make a profit? How many paintings on my Etsy store do I need to sell per month to support myself and quit my day job? Write out the numbers, analyze your spending habits, be real and make a six-month plan. Break your goals into four quarters per year, and then break it down into what you need to bring in each month. When you break it down, you realize that is isn't as scary as what it seemed to be in your head. If you don't feel strong in the finance department, there are so many reasonable money coaches out there. Perhaps you could go to the finance department at a local University and see if a Professor or student would be willing to tutor you and help you get organized. You have options, you just need to get creative and have the courage to ask for help.

Think, do, and say everything that will make you feel good about money, life, and love! All aspects of your life are intertwined and you have to be healthy and happy in all aspects of your life to receive abundance as well.

Believe this, write it on your mirror, have it by your bedside table, repeat it to yourself morning and night until you believe it in your core, in your soul; I am perfect, I love and value myself deeply. I am the best version of myself, and I am only getting better every day. I am doing more than enough. I am blessed.

111

2. Money Mindset Tools

I have read many books, taken many money courses and worked with great money and wealth coaches. Almost always, we over complicate our stories and our fears. It is only when we decide to take action steps that we can face the issues head on, make a plan and master our own financial issues. Think about it, when we go to a mall or walk into a store, we have billion dollar brands and corporations working against us. They spend a lot of time and money and people are hired as full-time employees to create an experience for us as consumers to feel a lack of something and in return we feel a need to buy a product in their store and in the moment. But, why? Because it is supposed to make us feel good. But does this impulse purchase really make us feel good if we can't afford it? Why do we splurge or spend frugally and get ourselves into trouble in the first place? My money coach taught me to keep a money journal and goes by one rule of thumb. Before any purchase, sit on it for 24 hours. If you still feel the same need or urgency then, buy it. But often, you won't feel the same need or level of urgency as you did in the moment.

In my money journal, every time I purchased something, I had to write about how it made me feel. For instance, drinks with friends made me feel free, excited, inspired and fun. She taught me though, that there are many other ways without spending money to feel this way. For instance, have friends over and cook dinner or host a potluck party. You save money and probably have even more fun on the couch kicking off your shoes than at a loud crowded bar downtown! You can find out more about working with Ashley and The Fiscal Femme on my website, BusyGirlDaily.com.

Here are a few simple busy girl tools that will help you shift your belief system and money fears:

- Be simple and light to receive money aka, don't overthink it!

- Expansion and growth are important for abundance. Never set limits or boundaries on yourself or your worth.

- Shift your fears about money to love and

appreciation for what you have, and for what money gives you. Freedom, ability to help others, travel, feeling empowered, etc.

- Do not ever doubt, question, or feel bad about what you want. There is so much abundance in this world, plenty to go around. There is so much room on top!

- Get comfortable with your money. Feel good paying bills, spending money, saving money, planning trips and what you will spend your money on. Start having fun with it!

- Have a date night with your money. Organize your bill pay, understand your credit score, your savings, your retirement funds, etc. Do research, set some goals. Open a bottle of wine, get your favorite take out, and have fun with it!

Print out the last six months of all your bank statements and all of your spending. With different colored highlighters, pick different categories (for example, gas, bill pay, cash at ATM, beauty, groceries, going out to dinner, etc.). Total your monthly expenses and analyze the average, this way you will be honest with yourself about your actual spending habits and understand clearly what could be worked on. You may be overspending or underspending in areas that you weren't aware of. For example, I was paying way more on monthly Uber rides than I realized. I was shocked!

- Find money mentors, or people you look up to who are successful and abundant. Learn from them, ask them to teach you and guide you. Be open about your goals and what you want to bring in.

- Write a story to yourself. If you had endless amounts of money, how would it make you feel? How would you spend your day? Write out your dream life, and read it back to yourself every evening before you fall asleep.

- You may have old limiting belief systems from your parents and upbringing that aren't even yours to keep. For example: "life is hard, you have to work hard to be successful, etc." Let go of these old belief systems; write them down and let them go. Physically burn your list and drop it in your fireplace. You have to deconstruct and let go of old belief systems that are not serving you in order to reconstruct and move forward.

- Increase the enjoyment of a physical thing in your life, not with cash, but with appreciation. For example, I appreciate that money and success allows me to live in this beautiful apartment and decorate it how I want.

- If you feel stuck in any particular area of your life (love, family, friends, health, etc.) your money will be stuck too. You have to feel complete and happy in all areas of your life in order to bring money and abundance into your life, and in order to keep growing it.

Start learning to live and spend below your means. You have to put something away each month to become responsible about money and spending habits.

· In order to have money, you have to love money. Have a deep love and appreciation for it. Change your feelings around money from fear to love. Shift these feelings and practice them daily until they are second nature.

· Find joy in paying bills, in being organized and responsible about your money, and in spending it. Love the relationship you have with your money. Work on it and grow it.

· Don't try to have too much control over your money, be light and easy about it. Feel good about saving, feel good about watching your money grow!

• Money is just energy. You are just energy. You have to align your energy with money by working on self-love, self-esteem and feeling good each day.

Busy Girl Tip: You can print this list and other Busy Girl activities on www.busygirldaily.com.

3. Redefining Failure and Failing Forward

"What we have once enjoyed we can never lose. All that we love deeply becomes a part of us." - **Helen Keller**

Most of us grew up being told to never quit, to never give up, to push and to fight until the end. Since a young age, this is something that I never understood. When I was a young girl, I was very curious, and I wanted to try everything. From soccer, to lacrosse, to woodworking, to baton twirling and even ballet, I tried it all. I was curious to see what they were all about, and to see whether any of them were for me. Luckily, I had parents who accepted my curiosity and my ADHD, and if I didn't want to go to soccer practice in the rain, I wouldn't go. It turns out, I hated sports, I loved ballet, and I really loved my woodworking class (even though I was the only girl in class). Around me though, I watched a lot of my peers being forced to go to piano lessons and soccer practice when they weren't feeling well, when it was raining and cold, and they were miserable doing it.

When I entered high school, I remember being challenged and judged for giving up so easily. During math class, I would stare at the ceiling, and even randomly circle A, B, C, or D when tests came around. I couldn't care less, and it showed. In English class, however, I was the first to show up, I was eager to receive the next assignment, and I truly thrived. These courses and lessons inspired me and made me feel alive. I excelled in some courses while almost failing out in others, and for some reason, at a young age I accepted that this was ok and that there was a lot more to life and success than the grades on my math tests.

Since a young age, we were taught a certain way, and the culture we live in today still supports the theory of never giving up and fighting until the end. Now, at 30-years-old, I look up to many successful entrepreneurs and authors. One of the themes that they all have in common is that they simply always follow their bliss. They don't push against things, and they give up easily when it feels like they are pushing against the natural flow of life. In Silicon Valley, they call this failing forward. It is actually something to strive for in order to be the best in your field, and necessary in order to be happy and to find your place in the world. The CEO of Whole Foods said in a recent interview that he hated reading in school. So at a young age, he decided that he would never pick up a book that he didn't want to read again. In college, that meant doing poorly in several classes, but he really didn't care. A 16-year-old intern of mine, who also recently gave a TED talk, was introduced as the average "C" student. Meanwhile, he is working on his third successful venture, and may very well be our next Steve Jobs. He does not let school or society judge him, or define his success.

Failing and quitting has always come with a negative connotation. However, I ask you to truly challenge this. Take away the shame and guilt and what others may think of you, and only do what feels right for you. I hate the word failing and quitting, because they feel so negative. Since quitting wasn't something that scared me or defined me, I knew I had to feel good about my choices and re-define the meaning of it. I decided to look at giving up and letting go of things as "letting them grow," instead. You see, if I didn't listen to my heart, I wouldn't have thrived in writing and learning about the things that I was most passionate about in school. If I didn't let go of my wedding planning career, I would have never launched my brands, or pushed myself to be a Huffington Post blogger or to write a book.

I use this tool in my personal life as well. When I let go of an ex-boyfriend, or a friend who was no longer healthy for me, I instead define these situations as "letting them grow." You have to let go of a situation or a person in your life, to let something bigger and better come in and grow. Instead of focusing on saying goodbye and bitter ends, I focus on the feeling of coming home to a better fitting person, place, career or circumstance in my life.

Despite all of the trials and errors, the giving up, the pushing harder, the failing forward, it all comes back to how you want to define your life, your purpose and your goals. It is all about perspective, and only you have the power to define your situations and circumstances. It is easy to feel negativity, guilt, pressure and pain, and sometimes it is harder to strive toward the good feeling thoughts, the appreciation, and the positivity. But we are all capable of being happy and finding our purpose. We are all capable of redefining the tougher circumstances in our lives and making them work for us. I ask you to go easy on yourself, and to love and honor the choices you make. It doesn't have to make sense to anyone but yourself. If you believe that life is happening for you and not to you, then you will never be a victim to anything that comes your way, and you are already winning.

Don't fall in love with one particular future or the way you think it should be. Be open to all opportunities that come your way, and never set limits on yourself. Life is filled with so many beautiful challenges and changes. When you are open to them, the

126

opportunities flow in much easier. So now I ask you, what are you going to quit today? Start failing forward, faster, and letting it grow!

Again, I want to ask you to re-define failure, quitting and what it means to you. If you look back at your life, when you quit and changed directions, was it for the best? Did you follow your heart, and did it lead you to bigger and better things? Do you wish you had quit sooner? The most difficult part of life is to let go of the oars and stop trying to steer the ship so directly. Most of us grew up setting limits on ourselves, and falling in love with the way we think life should be. But when you let go, when you allow, accept and realize that life is happening for you and not to you, you will start to connect with yourself and your world in a much deeper way. When you don't fall in love with one particular outcome, and are open and welcome to many changes on your path, the world will start to offer you more beautiful opportunities in love, health, abundance, and happiness.

4. Changing Your Perspective

"Your enemies are your best friends in disguise."

– Dr. Mindy Kopolow (Law of Attraction Expert)

Do you realize that your enemies, the most frustrating people in your life, are actually the most amazing teachers? Every difficult situation and person that we encounter in life, we actually created them ourselves in order to learn, expand, and grow. You see, challenges, and challenging people are brilliant gifts to help us grow. When you can truly understand this amazing fact, and shift your perspective when going through a hard time, your struggles in dealing with difficult people and situations will become more manageable. They may even become enjoyable if you can accept them simply as a part of life's lesson plan for you and necessary for the journey you are on. The negative people that show up in your life are only pushing you to expand, to be a stronger, better, wiser, and a more well-rounded person.

When you can accept and appreciate these hard times, and instead make the situation about you, what you are learning, and what you are getting out of it, it will actually give great meaning and purpose to each negative circumstance. Many of the most enlightened, happy and successful people in this world have actually seen the darkest of times. It is when you find value and lessons in the dark times, that you are closer to reaching your fullest potential. They actually might hold as much purpose, or the same as your best friend does. The most important tool that I can give to you is the idea that "it is all personal". It is all about you. The difficult people who show up in our lives, and the amazing ones too, they are simply a reflection of what you believe about yourself on the inside. The people and situations that show up in your life are mirroring your internal reality. They show up and put a spotlight on that thing that you might need to heal the most. This may be a very difficult realization, and you may put up a fight before accepting it. But one day, after the same issue, the same topic, and the same frustration shows up again in your life for the fifth time, after five different boyfriends, co-workers, or frenemies, you may start to pay attention to it.

You see, the same topics and the same struggles will come into our lives repeatedly until we choose to face the underlying issues that they are bringing up for us head on. Work through them and learn the lesson behind them. It is only once we do this that you have the opportunity to heal and release the person, the circumstance, and the lesson. This will allow room for personal growth, expansion, and will result in not attracting that same type of person into your life going forward, as they will no longer hold a purpose for you.

I have had several "teachers" in my life who have strongly tested my patience and my kindness. I have searched high and low for the answers as to why these people are in my life, yet it still took me time to get rid of them. In the moments when I am completely honest with myself, though, I realized what a beautiful teacher they were, only disguised as a horrible enemy. Although my anger and frustration with them was hard to deal with in the moment, I challenged myself to focus on the bigger picture, and realized that these situations were actually perfect teachers for me. They challenged me, made me tougher, made me question my judgement, my responsibility, my ability to succeed, my stability, my intelligence, and there was a major lack of respect. When I sit back and ponder all of this and I am truly honest with myself, it is my own stuff that I needed to work through, and that needed to be spotlighted for me in order to go within and heal. These people were pushing me to stand up, to defend and demand my respect, my judgement, and my choices in order to reach my fullest potential.

When I see how far I have come, and how confident I am since having been pushed by these circumstances, I can actually go into appreciation for the lessons that they have taught me. Although I do not have to like the people who showed up in my life, or the emotions and hardships that they put me through, I can now see the bigger picture and the lesson. I know that those people did hold a very important purpose in my life. In the past, when I found myself in a heated situation, and it made my blood boil, I would sit and say to myself as I look at the person who was driving me crazy, "Thank you for being my teacher, thank you for being my teacher, thank you for being my teacher." This helps me to stay calm and keep the focus on me and my growth and future rather than staying focused on them. It was a tender balance between appreciation and learning, while also sticking up for myself and standing my ground. When you find yourself in the thick of a difficult situation, it will feel like such a major waste of time and energy, yet the lesson will not go away until you heal the issue within yourself and learn the lesson.

Personally, I have come a long way from healing what I needed to heal, but I know that life has big plans for me. It is necessary to become the best version of myself, to become stronger, to demand more respect, to choose my words and my time wisely, and to always stay humble, kind, classy and respectful, even when I do not receive it from others. In the end in taking this approach, I can feel good about myself when I go to bed at night, I can rest easy and I can appreciate all of the ups and downs that life has to offer. I know that it is all working for us towards our greater good, even if we cannot understand it in the current moment. So I challenge you all to dig deep and find reason and greater meaning in these difficult situations. Always let the lesson be more important than the fight. Take it inward and make it about you. Always be the bigger person and focus on shifting your perspective from negative to positive. In the end, if you can think this way, you will always win. You will feel so good about yourself for being able to take a negative situation or person, and shift it into something very positive, meaningful and constructive in your life.

Letting go:

This ritual can be used if you are having repetitive thoughts or feelings about a certain situation or person. For me, I had a bad business relationship that

I really needed to end. It drained me of my energy and time and I really struggled with disconnecting from it. This practice is visualization, and its purpose is to return any unwanted energy to a person in your life, and to take back any energy that you have given away. This will create a release from you and something or someone that you may be holding onto in your past.

To begin: Close your eyes and visualize standing in front of the person or situation that you want to be disconnected from. Now, picture a rope of energy connecting from you to the other person or situation. Acknowledge and accept the other person or situation and send them love and forgiveness. Allow them to do the same to you. Then watch as a spiritual master/guide or angel, whatever you want to visualize walks between you offering peace to both of you and the situation. They acknowledge you and the other person and with a large gold sharp sword, they cut the energy rope between you two. After this, you take the disconnected piece of rope and turn it in towards you, and let it vanish into your system. You watch the other person do the same, bow to each other giving them their own energy back, separating and taking yours back as well. Then turn and walk away.

This practice focuses on taking back your energy, or any disconnect that may have occurred in your past. You can now breathe in deeply, relax, and know that you have restored your full energy and have disconnected from that person or situation that you felt you were energetically still connected to and being drained by. You will probably notice that you will think less about this person or situation, because you have internally released it and let it go. You have also demanded back your full power and energy, which you can now take with you and move on feeling complete. It may take several times, it may take a month or more to practice this, but eventually, you will take back all of your energy and cut ties with this person or situation and fully let it go. You can also make up your own rituals at home and give them meaning and purpose. Light a candle and burn a limiting belief and let it go, run in the pouring rain and start a new cleansing ritual, get creative and make up your own! You don't need to hire a coach or spend money or time waiting for someone to heal you, you can heal yourself. When you truly understand and own this, you take back your power and control over your own life, happiness and future.

5. Never feel lonely again

If you are feeling lonely, there are many methods to help you find love and comfort. I want you to realize that you can find love and comfort in nature and the world around you. If you are feeling lonely, you can ask the universe to provide you with love and comfort. You can take a walk in nature, and realize the beauty and love all around you. You can also look to any living creature, a plant, or an animal to fill yourself up with love and comfort. Go visit your local animal shelter and spend some time with a living animal that is also in need of love and comfort. The most important thing to remember is that you are loved and you are supported, even when you can't physically see it or feel the support around you, it is still there. You have so many options and there are so many possibilities to find love, peace and comfort when feeling alone. Go online and search the hashtag #busygirltribe and you will know that you are not alone. There are thousands of women going through the same journey that you are, and you are not alone. When others cannot love you or support you, keep in mind that they are hurting and struggling inside too. The more negative the behavior of a person, the more they are actually hurting inside. Have compassion and empathy for them and do not take it personally. It is never about you. Set healthy boundaries for yourself. Look instead to nature, to animals and to supportive people to fill up your love tank. Let the others go, it is all ok.

BUSY GIRL ACTIVITY 3

Meditation And Rituals For The Busy Girl

Mindfulness is similar to mediation, however you can do it while driving, while in a meeting, or home alone. This practice can take as little as one minute, or up to as long as you wish to stay with it. To start, ask yourself aloud, or in your head, "are ready to go into presence?" From there, focus on something living with a soft gaze. This could be a person, a pet, a plant, anything that is living. Going into presence is similar to beginning a mediation, start with a head to toe check in. Go from the top of your head, to the bottom of your feet. Feel or pay attention to any pain, sensitivity, pressure, or any feeling that you may be experiencing. I often use this practice when I have headache. Now, find an area that you want to pay attention to, (I usually start with my head) and offer kindness to the area you are focused on. Now, at first, this may be hard to wrap your mind around. For me, I imagine that a larger force, or vibration from the universe is assisting me in this process. The energy of kindness is being sent into my body, starting from the top of my head, and heading down to my toes. I usually sit and focus on the sensation that my body is feeling, and continue to offer kindness to that area of focus. I literally say, "kindness, kindness, kindness" over and over again in my head. The first few times I tried this, I felt nothing. However, when I got the hang of it, this practice started to energize and relax me. Literally, I felt more inspired, alert, and enthusiastic. Any time I need a little internal love or support, I know that I have this practice to turn to no matter how busy I am. You can practice meditation or presence at any time, whether you are feeling happy, sad, energized, stressed, tired, or sick. It will always elevate you, no matter what state you are in.

Meditation is also a beautiful practice. It cannot be done wrong, so do not overthink it. There are a million ways to practice mediation. Though, as someone who has very little patience and time, I try to make meditation as simple as possible. Dr. Mindy Kopolow showed me a very simple way to practice meditating. Set your alarm or phone to a five or ten-minute timer. Simply sit or lie down in a comfortable position and close your eyes. Focus first on relaxing your entire body from head to toe. Take deep belly breaths and count to ten. Inhale through the nose, and out through the mouth. When you find yourself more relaxed, I want you to focus on the number one. Say it over and over again in your head. During the next five or ten minutes, all you need to concentrate on is focusing on the word one. Naturally, other thoughts will come in. Don't push them out or get frustrated. Simply acknowledge them, put them in an imaginary cloud and watch them float away. Then, come back to the number one. Again, meditation cannot be done wrong, so don't over think it. The practice itself is calming and healing, even if you only can focus for thirty seconds. It is amazing to add this practice to your daily, or weekly routine, but I understand that it can be tough to find the time, or get into this habit so that is why I practice presence.

Your Busy Girl Action Plan & Closing:

I want to take a moment to thank and honor you for investing in yourself and your happiness. I hope you have enjoyed this journey and that it was simple and painless for you. Busy Girl's Guide is devoted to making "self-help" simple, easy and fun. I invite you to go easy on yourself, relax, invite some humor into your everyday and have more fun on your journey. I also want you to walk away with this mindset: I am released from my worries, my doubts and my fears. I am healed, I am complete, and I am whole. I have everything that I need within me, and I am ready to move forward honoring my power and my purpose.

KRISTINA D. TSIPOURAS

ABOUT THE AUTHOR

Kristina D. Tsipouras is a 31 year old Author and Entrepreneur living and loving life in Boston, Massachusetts. She lives with her boyfriend, and their beloved dog and cat, Maddie and Juliet. Kristina is a Huffington Post Blogger, Founder of Boston Business Women, Busy Girl Daily, and is the CEO of Moroccan Magic organic lip balms.

Find Kristina on Instagram & twitter:
@busygirlboston

www.busygirldaily.com

#BUSYGIRLTRIBE

BUSY GIRL APPROVED TOOLS & RESOURCES

Visit **www.busygirldaily.com** or google the methods below to find out more!

- Vision board

- Positive aspect list

- Focus wheel

- Feng shui

- Reiki

- Crystals

- Acupuncture

- Sound bath

- Aura photography

- Daily affirmations

- Deprivation tank

- Essential oils

- Rescue remedy

- Dry brushing

- Tumeric tea

- Abraham Hicks daily quotes

- TUT - Email from the Universe

- Hay House radio

- Abraham Hicks

- Gabrielle Bernstein

- Kriss Karr

- Thebachbook.com

- Orin and Daben meditations

- Oprah (Super Soul Sunday on OWN network)

- Arianna Huffington - THRIVE online course

- Mindyteacheslawofattraction.com

- Ashaisnow.com

- Abraham Hicks Youtube channel

- Bashaar

Other recommended books to continue your journey:

- You are a Badass, Jen Sincero

- Lucky Bitch, Denise Duffield-Thomas

- Ask and it is Given, Esther & Jerry Hicks

- A place of Yes, Bethenny Frankel

- Big Magic, Elizabeth Gilbert

Made in the USA
Middletown, DE
23 April 2016